# Black Stars in Orbit

# Black Stars in Orbit

## NASA'S
## AFRICAN AMERICAN
## ASTRONAUTS

*Khephra Burns and William Miles*

GULLIVER BOOKS
HARCOURT BRACE & COMPANY
*San Diego   New York   London*

ACKNOWLEDGMENTS

Khephra Burns and William Miles would like to thank astronauts Guion S. Bluford, Jr.;
Mae C. Jemison; Edward J. Dwight, Jr.; Robert H. Lawrence; Frederick D. Gregory;
Ronald E. McNair; Charles F. Bolden, Jr.; and Bernard Harris, Jr.

They wish to express their gratitude to Mrs. Barbara Lawrence, Mrs. Vance Marchbanks,
Dr. Jesco Von Puttkamer, Dr. Robert Shurney, Dr. Irene Long, Mr. Isaac Gillam IV,
and Dr. George Carruthers.

Special thanks to Nichelle Nichols and Dr. Curtis M. Graves.

And thanks in particular to their literary agents, Faith Childs and Edy Selman, and to their editors,
Liz Van Doren and Anne Davies, for all their patience and help.

————————

All photographs are courtesy of NASA except as noted. AP/Wide World Photos: p. 22, p. 23, p. 26.
Courtesy of Ethel M. Bolden: p. 59 (inset image). Courtesy of Georgia A. Dwight: p. 18.
Miles Educational Films: p. 17, p. 31 (inset image). Courtesy of National Archives: p. 1, p. 11, p. 12,
p. 14 (bottom image), p. 21 (both images). Naval Research Laboratory: p. 32 (both images). Courtesy
of Joan Vitale Strong: p. 63 (bottom image). Courtesy of Jannie K. Taylor: p. 54 (photo by
Franklin Elcock, Sr.). Courtesy of United States Air Force: p. 13, p. 14 (top image), p. 19, p. 25
(both images), p. 29.

————————

*Gulliver Books* is a registered trademark of Harcourt Brace & Company.

Library of Congress Cataloging-in-Publication Data
Burns, Khephra.
Black stars in orbit: NASA's African American astronauts/by Khephra Burns and William Miles.
—1st ed.
p.    cm.
"Gulliver books."
ISBN 0-15-200432-7     ISBN 0-15-200276-6 (pbk.)
1. African American astronauts—United States—Biography—Juvenile literature.
[1. Astronauts.   2. African-Americans—Biography.]
I. Miles, William, 1931–    . II. Title.
TL789.85.A1B87   1995
629.45'0092'273—dc20     [B]   93-44624

The text was set in Century Old Style.

Designed by Kaelin Chappell

*Printed in Singapore*

C  E  G  H  F  D
A  B  C  D  E  (pbk.)

# Contents

# PART ONE

# *Taking Flight*

# On the Wings of a Dream

T HE LONGING TO FLY, TO SOAR LIKE THE BIRDS, is one of the oldest and most deep-seated of human dreams and desires. Ancient Greek mythology tells of a master craftsman named Daedalus who constructed wings out of wax and feathers for himself and his son, Icarus. Trapped in an elaborate and winding maze on the Isle of Crete, they planned to use their wings to escape and return home to Athens and freedom. But young Icarus was overcome by the sheer exhilaration of flying and, although warned against it, flew too high and too close to the sun. The wax melted, his wings disintegrated, and he fell from the skies into the cold, churning sea below.

In African American folklore there's the story of Robbie Mc-Queen, Katie, old man Jacob King, and others from Africa who were brought to America as slaves and forced to labor on plantations in the Sea Islands off the coast of Georgia and South Carolina. One day when they were out in the fields, they decided they'd had enough of slavery. So they threw down their hoes and stopped working. The overseer got out his whip and was going to flog them, but before he could strike the first blow, they all rose up into the air like birds and flew back to Africa where they could be free.

All over the world, in almost every culture, there are ancient tales of ships that sail through the air, winged horses, and magic flying carpets. These myths have evolved from a common dream. And in every age since human beings first gazed up into the heavens, the dream of flight has meant freedom. But only in this century has that dream become a reality. In 1903 the Wright brothers, Orville and Wilbur, achieved the first successful powered flight of an airplane. In 1958 America established the National Aeronautics and Space Administration (NASA), and within eleven years NASA succeeded in landing the first men on the moon. But it took decades and much effort on the parts of thousands of men and women for the first African American astronaut to go into space. As of 1993 there have been six African Americans aboard spacecraft and innumerable others involved behind the scenes of America's space program.

African Americans have made important contributions to the development of space flight. They have pioneered new technologies, and like the Africans in the folktale who rose into the air like birds to claim their freedom, African Americans have risen from the cotton fields of slavery to soar beyond the wildest dreams of their parents and grandparents. They have reached the heights of scientific achievement despite the racial discrimination that often denied them the same opportunities other Americans took for granted. Because of them, we live in a time when African American men and women are free to explore new worlds and make exciting new discoveries.

The first African American to venture into space was Colonel Guion S. Bluford, Jr. At 2:32 A.M. on August 30, 1983, Colonel Bluford took his place in history beside other African American pioneers when the Space Shuttle *Challenger* lifted off from the Kennedy Space Center in Florida on mission STS-8. The initials *STS* stand for Space Transportation System, the official name of the Space Shuttle, and the *8* means that this flight was the eighth Space Shuttle mission. (If

*The historic launch of STS-8.*
*The Space Shuttle* Challenger *lifts*
*off at 2:32 A.M. on August 30, 1983.*

a mission requires more than one flight, each flight will have a letter after the mission number as well.) STS-8 was also the first-ever nighttime launch of a shuttle. Thousands of people, who had come from all over the country to see the historic launch, stood in the rain rather than miss it. They waited nervously for hours in the dark and dismal weather as the countdown was stopped and then started again. Then, when the countdown reached T–9—only nine seconds left to go before liftoff—the weather broke, the rain stopped, and a hole opened up in the clouds to reveal the starry sky. Anticipation and excitement mounted as the countdown grew closer . . . eight, seven, six, five, four, three, two, one. . . . Ignition! Suddenly, the earth shook and a fiery brilliance lit up the night, almost turning night into day. The blast from the solid rocket boosters could be

*Guion S. Bluford, Jr., the first African American to journey into space*

seen as far away as North Carolina, five hundred miles up the eastern coast of the United States.

Guion Stewart Bluford, Jr., or Guy, as his friends call him, was born November 22, 1942, in Philadelphia, Pennsylvania. As a youngster Guy loved building model airplanes and read everything he could get his hands on to learn what makes them fly. By the time he reached the seventh grade, he had developed a passion for math and the sciences. That was also about the time he decided he would pursue a career in aeronautical engineering.

The Space Shuttle, still attached to its two solid rocket boosters and its external fuel tank, shoots through the sky moments after a successful takeoff from the Kennedy Space Center in Florida. February 1984

From the Space Shuttle, astronauts look down to see views like this one of the sun shining over the Pacific Ocean and the cloud-covered Andes Mountains of South America.

Like millions of other young African Americans with lofty goals, Guy encountered high-school guidance counselors who tried to discourage him from pursuing his dream. One of those guidance counselors advised him to settle for a career as a carpenter or an auto mechanic instead. The hidden message was that, as a black person, he didn't have the intelligence to become an aeronautical engineer. But the counselors' skepticism only made Guy work that much harder to prove them wrong. He got into Pennsylvania State University and graduated four years later with a bachelor of science degree in aerospace engineering. At the same time he completed the Air Force Reserve Officers' Training Corps (ROTC) Program at Penn State. After graduation Guy went right into the Air Force, and within a year he had earned his wings. Colonel Bluford went on to log more than five thousand hours of jet flight time and to earn his Ph.D. in aerospace engineering with a minor in laser physics.

Then in the mid 1970s Colonel Bluford joined NASA and became one of a new breed of astronauts known as mission specialists. Mission specialists are responsible for conducting all of the scientific and engineering experiments aboard the shuttle. As part of the five-man crew of STS-8, Colonel Bluford carried out medical experiments that are only possible in the weightless conditions of space. These experiments may eventually yield new drugs or even cures for some diseases. Colonel Bluford was also responsible for deploying a $45 million communications satellite for the government of India. The satellite, which had been carried into space aboard the shuttle, had to be released carefully into its proper orbit in order for it to be of any use to India or to anyone on earth; otherwise it would end up as $45 million worth of useless space junk.

Guy Bluford's responsibilities were great, but the personal rewards were also great. The experience of floating weightless in space and of seeing the earth we live on, alone in the vast black expanse of space—these are experiences that only a very few people have had in the history of human existence. If Guy Bluford had listened to those who told him what he couldn't do, he would never have become one of those rare few we call astronauts.

*Mae C. Jemison, the first African*
*American woman to travel into space*

It was ten years from the time of Colonel Bluford's first flight until an African American woman ventured into space. NASA's first black woman astronaut, Dr. Mae C. Jemison, made her historic first flight aboard the Space Shuttle *Endeavour* on September 12, 1992. She was part of the seven-member crew of STS-47 that carried Spacelab-J into orbit in a joint venture between the United States and Japan. Spacelab-J is a pressurized laboratory, about the size of a city bus, that can be fitted into the cargo bay of the Space Shuttle. Over the course of the seven-day mission, the crew lived and worked in Spacelab-J, conducting forty-three major experiments while orbiting the earth at nearly eighteen thousand miles per hour.

After STS-47 landed, Dr. Jemison returned to her hometown of Chicago. There, eight thousand schoolchildren attended a homecoming party and celebrated her accomplishment, just as their parents, grandparents, and great-grandparents had celebrated the accomplishments of earlier pioneer aviators.

# Birth of the Black Eagles

## *Fighter Pilots of World War II*

URING THE EARLY TWENTIETH CENTURY FLYING captured the imagination of America's youth, and black youths were as eager as anyone to take to the skies. America made heroes of Charles Lindbergh, who made the first solo flight from New York to Paris, and of Eddie Rickenbacker, the World War I ace fighter pilot. African Americans also had their heroes—young men including Dale White and Chauncey Spencer, who flew from Chicago to Washington, D.C., to demonstrate to the government and the nation that black people could fly. Charles A. Anderson, known as Chief Anderson, became the first African American to hold a commercial pilot's license. And Willa B. Brown, the first black woman to hold a commercial pilot's license, not only flew airplanes but also operated a flying school near Chicago.

When the United States entered World War II, young African Americans from all over the country went to their local Army recruiters and tried to sign up to be fighter pilots. America had not yet established the United States Air Force as a separate branch of the armed services, so young men who wanted to be fighter pilots enlisted as aviation cadets in the Army Air Force. But the Army did

*Judge William Hastie, civilian aide
to Secretary of War Henry Stimson*

just about everything it could to discourage young African Americans who wanted to fly.

The armed forces during World War II were still racially segregated, as was the rest of American society; the military expected black men to cook, dig ditches, and clean up after whites, not to serve their country as fighter pilots. Dissatisfied with this, the National Association for the Advancement of Colored People (NAACP), the Urban League, and other civil rights organizations began to put pressure on the government to allow African Americans to fight for their country and to become pilots and officers. A black judge, Judge William Hastie, was appointed civilian aide to the

*Black Eagles lined up for inspection at the flying school for Negro Air Corps Cadets, Tuskegee, Alabama*

secretary of war. It was Judge Hastie's job to make recommendations to the secretary of war about how to integrate black people into the armed services and make better use of their talents and skills. But the secretary of war, Henry Stimson, resisted Judge Hastie's recommendations in every way he could. Undaunted, Judge Hastie and the various civil rights organizations kept up the pressure, and the president's wife, First Lady Eleanor Roosevelt, even got involved in the push for equal opportunity for African Americans in the military. Finally, a program to teach black recruits to fly was set up at the Tuskegee Army Airfield in Tuskegee, Alabama, and the first lady visited the airfield and went for an airplane ride with a black pilot just to show the nation that she believed black pilots could fly as well as anyone.

*Pilots from the 332d Fighter Group,
15th Army Air Force, huddle next to
a P-51 in Italy. September 1944*

The young black men who took part in the training program were under tremendous pressure to succeed. Secretary of War Henry Stimson and others in the military hoped the Tuskegee Experiment, as the program was known, would fail. The young pilots knew that they were representing their race and that if they failed, their failure would be taken as proof that blacks could not compete in a white man's world. Despite this pressure they not only proved that they could learn to fly but they excelled, mastering aerobatic maneuvers that were considered to be impossible with the airplanes they were flying.

Reluctantly, the military organized the young black pilots into the 99th Pursuit Squadron, the 332d Fighter Group, and the 477th Bombardment Group. The 99th and the 332d were sent overseas

*Lieutenant Lee A. Archer standing beside his P-51 in Italy, 1945. Having shot down five enemy aircraft in aerial combat, Lieutenant Archer should have been recognized as an "ace" pilot, but in the 1940s the Army Air Force would only give him credit for downing four and a half enemy aircraft.*

**Keep us flying!**

**BUY WAR BONDS**

*This poster featuring an African American pilot was used to sell war bonds in black communities like Harlem during World War II.*

and given the chance to prove themselves in combat, but still they were discriminated against and repeatedly put at a disadvantage by the white military establishment. During their service in Africa, while attached to a white group for combat, members of the 99th were ignored at precombat meetings; precise information about routes and targets was withheld from them; and even though they flew more missions and longer hours than their white counterparts, they were accused by white officers of lacking the stamina, reflexes, and intelligence of the white pilots.

Still, they sought out the enemy in the skies over North Africa and Italy. Young African American men like Lieutenant Lee "Buddy" Archer and his flamboyant wingman, Lieutenant Wendell O. Pruitt; Lieutenants Roscoe Browne, Clarence "Lucky" Lester, and others— some of them barely out of their teens—downed dozens of enemy aircraft in aerial dogfights. Their motto was Live in Fame or Go Down in Flames. Flying propeller-driven P-51 Mustangs, the Tuskegee Airmen, as they would later be known, shot down some of Germany's first jet fighters. They escorted bombers deep into Germany and never lost a single bomber to the enemy. They even sank a German destroyer escort with nothing more than machine-gun fire, something no other fighter group had ever accomplished. The Army did not want to give them credit for sinking the ship and would have liked to have denied their achievement, but cameras mounted on the wings of their P-47 Thunderbolts had recorded the incident on film through the massive barrage of gunfire the destroyer had sent up to try to shoot the men down.

Tuskegee's heroic black fighter pilots became the scourge of the skies over the Mediterranean. At the same time, they served on the front lines in the battle for racial justice and equal opportunity for black people at home in America and helped to prepare the military for the black pilots and black astronauts who would follow.

# Soaring Higher

## *Black Pilots Look to the Moon*

**T**ODAY THE TUSKEGEE AIRMEN ARE RECOGNIZED as national heroes, but in 1951 their exploits were still too little known for them to serve as role models for young black Americans interested in joining the Air Force. A noted sculptor today, Edward J. Dwight, Jr., was one of those young men. He had two consuming passions back then: art and aviation. Raised on a small farm near Kansas City, Kansas, he became interested in flying after he witnessed a P-39 aircraft crash at an airport about a mile from his home. Only ten years old at the time, Ed Dwight decided that he could do much better than the pilot who had crashed. He decided then that he would learn to fly.

Ed Dwight had graduated from high school and was attending a small junior college in Kansas City when he started going down to the local Air Force recruiting office every day to ask for an application for pilot training. And every day he was told the same thing— the Air Force was not letting his kind in. He was told this even though President Harry S. Truman had ordered the desegregation of the armed services in 1948. Dwight wrote to Washington and was

*Captain Edward J. Dwight, Jr., made history as the first African American to be selected for astronaut training. Today, as an acclaimed sculptor, he records history in his art.*

told that an aviation cadet evaluation team would be visiting his junior college campus.

*What I did not know at the time was there was a move afoot to recruit black pilots. Thirty-three of us from the college were sent to Denver [by the aviation cadet evaluation team] in 1951 . . . to Lowry Air Base to take the exam. Now, you have to understand that I was possessed with this airplane stuff, that I had been taking sample tests for pilot training ever since I was a junior in high school. You go to the library and they have these sample tests that they give you. They have math tests, they have physics tests, acceleration tests, the actual problems. I had been unwittingly working toward taking the real tests, playing this imaginary pilot guy, you know?*

*Edward Dwight at Reese Air Force
Base in Lubbock, Texas, in 1954*

*So all of us went, thirty-three of the most macho dudes on campus. And I came back as the only one to pass. Well, everybody got really upset about this. The fix was in, man. Dwight passes, none of the rest of us. Dwight's black, and I mean, something's wrong with this. But nobody had thought about the fact that I had practiced. I just zoomed right through the test because it was the same test I'd got out of these books.*

—ED DWIGHT

Dwight joined the Air Force two years later.

In 1961 Captain Dwight, now an Air Force jet pilot and flight instructor with a degree in aeronautical engineering from Arizona State University, received a letter from President John F. Kennedy

*Captain Dwight at Edwards Air Force Base in California in 1963*

offering him the opportunity to train to join the recently established NASA and become the first black astronaut. Captain Dwight was in high spirits when he showed the letter to his commanding officer.

*I said, "Do you know what this means?" And he said, "No." I said, "If I do this, I get a chance to be on the cover of* Ebony *magazine." And he looked at me with the strangest face. "What's* Ebony *magazine?"*

*So I got duly excited about it. And . . . against everybody's advice and wishes, I went on and sent my information in. In the fourteen years I was in the service, I never saw the Air Force react so swiftly. Within a couple of days I was sent to Edwards Air Force Base for an evaluation. And I knew full well that the plan was in place, that if, in fact, I did succeed and didn't fall on my face, that there was going to be some move afoot to line me up so that I would be on one of the lunar missions.*

*Kennedy had this dream of having a black and an Asian on the first
moon mission.*

*Because I kind of knew, it allowed me to take all that gaff that I was
getting down there. Because they did not want me down there. I heard
statements about it, how a certain high-ranking officer called in several
of the staff of the test pilot school and made a comment . . . that "Washington is trying to cram a nigger down our throats, and we don't want
that nigger to graduate, because if he graduates it'll hurt this program
and will destroy everything you people have been putting together."*

—ED DWIGHT

The officer referred to by Captain Dwight was Colonel Charles
Yeager, who had been the first test pilot to fly faster than the speed
of sound and who was the commandant of the Aerospace Research
Pilot School. According to Dwight, Yeager tried to get him to resign
several times. At one point Colonel Yeager had Dwight called into
his office and asked, "Who got you into this school? Was it the
NAACP, or are you some kind of black Muslim out here to make
trouble? . . . Why in hell would a colored guy want to go into space
anyway? As far as I'm concerned, there'll never be one to do it. And
if it was left to me, you guys wouldn't even get a chance to wear an
Air Force uniform." There were even veiled threats. Dwight recalled
Yeager once told him, "Ed, those people in Washington don't know
what we're doing down here. They could get you killed."

*I represented an incredible fear that Kennedy was going to be like
Branch Rickey and turn the space program into what Branch Rickey
did to baseball. And I was kind of like Jackie Robinson, and I was going
to be the experiment. The bigger fear with the integration of any area of
our society has always been not so much the first black person who
moves into the neighborhood or sport or what have you, but the numbers
of black people who follow, turning the neighborhood black. The fact of
the matter is, when you look at the basic requirements to be an astronaut, it eliminated a lot of people, a lot of minorities. You had to be
under thirty, you had to have an engineering degree or a degree in
natural science, and most blacks didn't have that. And then you had to
have over two thousand hours of jet time, and of course, they didn't let
blacks fly jets for an awful long time.*

*Captain Dwight in a class at the aerospace research pilot program. The instructor is using an astroglobe.*

*Captain Dwight shows a model of an F-104 to children at Edwards Air Force Base.*

*Captain Dwight's sentiments reflected the frustration felt by many blacks in the 1950s and 1960s when civil rights marches, freedom rides, and sit-ins swept through the South. Speaking out in cities from Atlanta and Montgomery to Washington, D.C., Dr. Martin Luther King, Jr., gave voice to the disaffection black people were feeling and led them in their struggle to attain equal rights.*

*And so, you add up all these factors, you end up here with a kind of oddball set of credentials that one has to have. From a black perspective, it was a strange set of credentials that nobody would go out and get on his own.*

—ED DWIGHT

With President Kennedy's assassination on Friday, November 22, 1963, Dwight's hopes of ever going into space began to fade. When Dwight arrived at work the following Monday he received orders shipping him out to Germany. He was told that he was going to be a liaison officer for the German test pilot school and space program. But the Germans didn't have a space program. Dwight went straight to the White House but was told there was nothing anyone could do for him. He was never officially notified that he was

*At the same time that Martin Luther King, Jr., was leading the civil rights movement in the South, Malcolm X, a minister of the Nation of Islam, galvanized the residents of cities throughout the North, speaking eloquently of the need for change in the North as well as the South.*

no longer in the space program, but by order of President Johnson, Dwight was effectively transferred out of the astronaut training program.

*So I was asked to go quietly. But before I went I had to write a big report telling the president what it was like, outlining what the next Negro who got the opportunity would have to bring to the job that I didn't. And I said that they had complained that I was undereducated, yet I had the same degrees that everybody else had. Apparently, somehow, their bachelor's degrees were worth more than my bachelor's degree, so if you're black, you have to have a doctorate. You also have to be a fighter pilot, you've got to understand how to fly. And the last words in my report were . . . "In other words, he's got to be Super Nigger."*

—ED DWIGHT

In 1967, three and a half years after Dwight was forced out of the astronaut training program, Air Force Major Robert H. Lawrence became America's first black astronaut designee. This meant that he had successfully completed the Air Force's astronaut training program, had been selected as an astronaut, and was awaiting a mission. Major Lawrence was an aerospace research pilot in the Manned Orbiting Laboratory (MOL) Program, which the Air Force operated independently of NASA. The MOL was going to orbit the earth with two men on board for a month, conducting surveillance for the military. Lawrence had twice applied to NASA, which was actively looking for qualified candidates for astronaut training in the mid 1960s. But despite his qualifications, which included a Ph.D. in physical chemistry and more than two thousand hours of jet-flying time, NASA had refused him both times. So he applied to the Air Force's Aerospace Research Pilot School and was accepted, becoming the only United States astronaut with a Ph.D. at that time.

On Friday, June 30, 1967, the Air Force held a press conference in El Segundo, California, to announce the selection of Major Robert Lawrence and three others—Major Donald H. Peterson, Major James A. Abrahamson, and Lieutenant Colonel Robert T. Herres—as its newest crop of astronauts. During the press conference, an interviewer commented, "Major Lawrence, I think most people feel that this is an historic step, that a Negro has been picked as an astronaut or an aerospace research pilot. Do you yourself feel that this is a tremendous step forward in racial relations?"

Major Lawrence chose his words very carefully. "No, I don't think it is especially a tremendous step forward. I think it's just another one of the things that we look forward to in this country with respect to progress in civil rights. Nothing dramatic has happened. . . . It's just a normal progression. . . ."

It was obvious from the film coverage of the press conference that Major Lawrence was uncomfortable with such close scrutiny by the media, which might interpret his confidence or pride as arrogance, or any statement about race as a sign of militancy.

*Exactly what kinds of problems an individual faces is kind of hard to define at this stage. I would say that many of the problems that are faced*

*Major Robert H. Lawrence climbing into the cockpit of an F-104 at Edwards Air Force Base in 1967*

*Major Lawrence with (left to right) Lieutenant Colonel Robert T. Herres, Major Donald H. Peterson, and Major James A. Abrahamson at the press conference on June 30, 1967, announcing that the four had been named to the Manned Orbiting Laboratory Program*

*At the close of Major Lawrence's funeral on December 12, 1967, Air Force bearers carry his flag-draped coffin out of First Unitarian Church, Chicago.*

*by a large number of Negroes in this country I have faced, yes. I think perhaps I've been a lot more fortunate than many in that several of the people who are responsible for my training just happened to be at the right place at the right time and supplied me with the necessary motivation and the background that I needed.*

—ROBERT LAWRENCE

Major Lawrence certainly faced less overt discrimination at the Aerospace Research Pilot School than Captain Dwight had, but years later Major Lawrence's wife hinted that her husband had also felt less than welcome there at times.

*I think because of the controversy that surrounded Dwight not being selected, that when we got to Edwards [Air Force Base] there had been a change in command, and I think the word had gone out that there were to be no such difficulties. So there were, officially, no difficulties.*

—BARBARA LAWRENCE

Part of the training for the MOL program was proficiency training in the F-104, a jet plane that could fly at twice the speed of sound, more than fourteen hundred miles an hour. The F-104 was sometimes described in press reports as "a missile with a man in it." On December 8, 1967, Major Lawrence was killed when the F-104 he was riding in crashed on landing at Edwards Air Force Base in California. Major Harvey J. Royer, who was flying the plane, ejected and was injured but survived. Major Lawrence, who was sitting in the backseat, also ejected, but Lawrence's parachute did not open. Many people feel that the investigation into the crash never gave a satisfactory explanation why one man's chute opened and the other man's did not.

*After Bob was killed I got a letter from some irate citizen that said they were glad he was dead because now there would be no coons on the moon. Mixed in with the sympathy cards, every once in a while you'd open an envelope and there would be a letter or a note saying how happy they were that the event had taken place.*

—BARBARA LAWRENCE

# Visions of Spaceflight

*On the Ground at NASA*

**M**ORE THAN TEN YEARS WOULD PASS BEFORE another African American was selected for astronaut training. But progress was being made—if not into space, at least into places of importance behind the scenes of America's space program. In just eight years of manned spaceflight, starting with Alan Shepard's fifteen-minute Mercury flight in 1961, NASA succeeded in landing the first men on the moon—Neil Armstrong and Edwin Aldrin. That was in 1969. Though there were no black astronauts among that elite corps of moon walkers, black doctors, scientists, and research engineers took some of the giant steps forward in the design of technology required by the astronauts.

As early as 1962 Colonel Vance Marchbanks had worked on the launch that put the first American astronaut into orbit around the earth. Colonel Marchbanks, a former Tuskegee Airman, had served as group surgeon with the 332d Fighter Group in Italy during World War II. In addition to logging more than fourteen hundred hours of flying time with further tours of duty in Korea and Okinawa, Colonel Marchbanks became a pioneer in the field of aeromedical research and, later, aerospace medicine. His prominence in the field

*Colonel Marchbanks played an important role at NASA in the 1960s. When John Glenn circled the earth in the* Friendship 7 *capsule, becoming the first American to orbit the earth in space, Marchbanks monitored Glenn's respiration, pulse, temperature, and heartbeat from a base in Kano, Nigeria. Marchbanks was responsible for making sure that Glenn was not experiencing any severe physical stress that might require the mission to be aborted.*

eventually led to his appointment by NASA as chief flight surgeon to astronaut John Glenn and one of eleven specialists responsible for monitoring Glenn's vital signs during the history-making Mercury mission, February 20, 1962. When NASA then set its sights on a moon landing, Colonel Marchbanks directed the medical and safety tests on the moon suits to be worn by the Apollo astronauts.

Aerospace engineer Dr. Robert Shurney is another one of those pioneers whose contributions to the development of sophisticated space technology helped to make America a world leader in the exploration of space. Dr. Shurney's design of tools and techniques for living and working in the weightless conditions of space made it possible for astronauts to stay up for days and weeks at a time. In space something as simple and natural as eating can be difficult and even dangerous. Although some foods such as apples or bananas can be eaten just as they are eaten on earth, others have to be contained to keep them from floating away. Water, or any other liquid, will float right out of a glass and form thousands of globules; eventually it might get into the controls and other equipment and possibly cause a disaster. To solve this problem, Dr. Shurney designed special zero-gravity utensils and trays that keep food from floating away. Dr. Shurney came up with the idea that most foods would have to come from a bottle or similar container, and that the astronaut would have to suck the food or liquid through a small tube.

Dr. Shurney also designed the lightweight aluminum tires used on the lunar rover that the astronauts of the Apollo 15 mission first drove around while on the moon.

*There were a lot of things we didn't know about the lunar surface. We didn't know the dust profile. And so we took from the information that we were able to obtain and eventually came up with the idea of the chevrons that are on the lunar rover wheel. We designed it in such a way that it would keep the dust off of the crewmen and they could see where they were going. . . . [The wheels] left a trail like a rooster's tail. That's where we got the idea.*

—DR. ROBERT SHURNEY

Because there is no atmosphere on the moon, and no wind or rain, the tracks left in the lunar dust by Dr. Shurney's moon buggy will remain there forever, just as they are.

Astronaut Charles M. Duke, Jr., one of the members of the Apollo 16 lunar landing mission, standing beside the moon buggy on the moon. April 1972

Dr. Robert Shurney in 1989 with a model of the moon buggy that he helped design

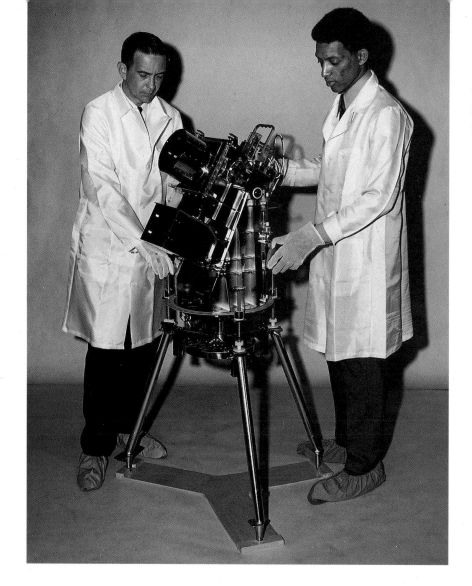

*William Conway and Dr. George Carruthers in 1972 with the ultraviolet camera they designed for use on NASA's lunar missions*

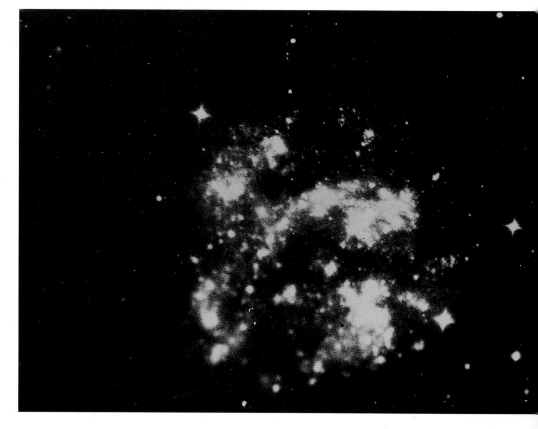

*This far-ultraviolet photograph of the Large Magellanic Cloud was taken during the Apollo 16 mission to the moon using the ultraviolet camera developed by Dr. Carruthers. The Large Magellanic Cloud is the galaxy nearest our Milky Way galaxy.*

Dr. Shurney was not the only black scientist to invent something that went to the moon with the Apollo astronauts. Dr. George R. Carruthers developed a combination telescope and camera that the astronauts who went to the moon used to take pictures of the earth, constellations, and galaxies, including Andromeda and the Magellanic Clouds. Because there is no atmosphere on the moon, there is also no smog or haze or anything else to obstruct the view of these distant stars and galaxies. And so, when the astronauts looked through Dr. Carruthers's telescope camera on the moon, their view was much clearer and extended many, many times farther than the view through the best telescope on earth.

George Carruthers got his first telescope when he was just ten years old. He became so fascinated with the stars that he taught himself the basics of astronomy—the location, magnitude, and distance of all the major constellations, how stars and galaxies form, and how to analyze the spectrum of their light for information about their composition. Armed with this knowledge, he was able to breeze through the University of Illinois. Dr. Carruthers is now a senior astrophysicist at the Naval Research Laboratory (NRL), where he is head of the ultraviolet measurements group. For more than twenty years, Dr. Carruthers has conducted experiments and observations in ultraviolet astronomy using rockets and space vehicles to take his telescopic cameras into space, where they can get a clear, unobstructed view of the stars and other celestial phenomena.

The contributions of scientists like Dr. Carruthers to the space program helped NASA to see that there was more to the space age than just exploration. There were things that scientists could do in space that couldn't be done on earth. Along with Colonel Marchbanks and Dr. Shurney, Dr. Carruthers no doubt also helped NASA to realize that there were qualified African American men and women out there who could be of tremendous benefit to the space program if they were just given the chance.

# PART TWO

# *Journey into Space*

# Counting Down

## *The Search for NASA's First Black Stars*

IN THE MID 1970S NASA BEGAN GEARING UP FOR A new kind of space program. Like the pioneers who explored America just a few hundred years ago, NASA's early astronauts had ventured out to explore new territory. But the time had come for others to follow those space pioneers and begin to make use of some of the rich resources and potential for industry that had been discovered in space. The new space program would explore opportunities for the development of new technologies in communications, medicine, weather surveillance, agriculture, and many other areas that would be of tremendous benefit to everyone right here on earth. For that, the space program would require a new kind of astronaut—men and women who would not necessarily fly the spaceship but could work as scientists aboard it once it was in orbit.

The new space program also required a new spaceship: one designed to carry larger numbers of scientists and a laboratory into space; one that could be launched like a rocket and could land like a plane rather than splashing down in the ocean with its crew and equipment the way previous generations of spacecraft had. This would be a spaceship that could be launched over and over again,

*NASA's new Space Shuttle was designed to be able to orbit the earth and then to return, landing with its passengers and equipment intact so both could participate in further missions.*

almost as regularly as a shuttle bus. NASA planned to call this new spacecraft the Space Shuttle.

In July 1976 NASA announced that it was going to select a new corps of astronauts to participate in the Space Shuttle program, and that applications from qualified candidates of all races and both genders were being accepted. But by February 1977, eight months into its yearlong recruitment drive, NASA had received only a hundred applications from women and fewer than thirty-five from minorities, none of whom were qualified. NASA didn't understand why more women and minorities were not responding to its call for applicants.

*NASA administrator Isaac Gillam IV and Nichelle Nichols posing in 1977 with a model of the new Space Shuttle as it would appear at liftoff, attached to its rocket boosters and external fuel tank*

NASA brought in a consultant—someone who was neither a scientist nor an astronaut. She was actress Nichelle Nichols, best known for her role as Communications Officer Lieutenant Uhura on the popular television series "Star Trek." She was already under contract with NASA to assist in developing symposiums for minority youths. NASA officials confided in Ms. Nichols about their concern that they were not getting the response they had hoped for from minorities and women, and they asked her why she thought NASA was having this problem. Nichols told them that, basically, minorities and women didn't believe that NASA was serious about recruiting them. NASA had had five recruitment drives before this one and each time had said that anyone who was qualified could apply—but qualified minority and women applicants were never chosen. So minorities and women who were qualified probably were not applying now because they felt it would just be a waste of their time. NASA officials said that this time they were serious, that they really did want minorities and women to be involved in the space program.

Nichols believed them, but she didn't see right away how she personally could be of much help to them in rectifying the problem. But that was before she fully realized the tremendous influence she had on people as Lieutenant Uhura of the Starship *Enterprise*.

*I wanted to see that we had men and women in the Space Shuttle. I had a vested interest, because I wanted to see that our "Star Trek" universe lived: men and women of all colors working together. So when NASA asked me, "How can we get people to apply?" I said, "I think you need to get someone immediately with credibility and high visibility, so that they [can] see them on television and in the newspapers and ads . . . and do a complete media blitz with people whom they would believe." And they said, "Who?" I said, "Bill Cosby, Coretta King . . ." Then NASA said, "How about Lieutenant Uhura?"*

—NICHELLE NICHOLS

What better spokesperson could NASA possibly find to help it recruit minorities and women than the only black female crew member of television's most famous spaceship, the Starship *Enterprise?* For the next four months Nichols traveled the country, speaking at universities and conventions of scientists and engineers and talking about NASA's new recruiting efforts on "Good Morning America" and other TV talk shows. NASA even put together a TV ad with Nichelle Nichols as Lieutenant Uhura that aired in March and April of 1977. Surrounded by models of the Space Shuttle and the *Enterprise*, Nichols encouraged qualified minorities and women to apply to NASA.

*In 1977 Nichelle Nichols appeared in a NASA television commercial as Lieutenant Uhura of "Star Trek." This time her mission was to recruit minorities and women for NASA's Space Shuttle program.*

*Hi, I'm Nichelle Nichols. Kind of looks like when I was Uhura on the starship* Enterprise, *doesn't it? Well, now there's a twentieth-century* Enterprise, *an actual space vehicle built by NASA and designed to put us in the business of space, not merely space exploration. NASA's* Enterprise *is a space shuttlecraft, built to make regularly scheduled runs into space and back. Now the shuttle will be taking scientists and engineers, men and women of all races, into space, just like the astronaut crew on the starship* Enterprise. *So that is why I'm speaking to the whole family*

*NASA's first black astronaut trainees: Ron McNair, Guy Bluford, and Fred Gregory. January 1978*

*of humankind, minorities and women alike. If you qualify and would like to be an astronaut, now is the time. This is your NASA.*

—NICHELLE NICHOLS

Applications from minorities and women skyrocketed. NASA received over 8,000 applications in all, 1,649 of them from women and over a thousand from minorities. From their ranks came the first shuttle astronauts, including six women, three African Americans, and an Asian American.

*Ron McNair, Guy Bluford, and Fred Gregory were the three black men that were selected. Those are my astronauts. I had contacted Ron McNair personally. I had sent contacts to Guy Bluford. And wonder of all wonders, Fred Gregory had heard me on a television talk show.*

—NICHELLE NICHOLS

*Ron McNair, Fred Gregory, and Guy Bluford, dressed in high-altitude pressure*
*suits, on their orientation tour at Johnson Space Center in Texas. January 1978*

Fred Gregory, Guy Bluford, and Ron McNair arrived at NASA in January 1978. After two weeks spent visiting and observing NASA's various installations, they went into a training program to acquire the basic skills they would need to do their job as astronauts. Their program included parasailing off the coast of Florida to learn how to work with parachutes, how to land in the water as well as on land, and how to survive in an open raft in the sea for several days. They also had to learn such things as emergency escape procedures for exiting a space vehicle on the launchpad. Then they learned about spaceflight, orbital mechanics, and important theories and aspects of technology that make up the basic body of knowledge required of all astronauts.

*During a survival school course for new astronauts at Vance Air Force Base in Oklahoma, Ron McNair braces himself for a simulated aircraft "ejection." McNair's seat will rise rapidly on a rail, thus simulating the experience of an aircraft ejection. August 1978*

After they finished one year of basic astronaut training, they advanced to training in specific systems, including the shuttle's computer hardware and software, its heat shield, and its satellite deployment and retrieval systems. They also began training for specific missions they would eventually fly, rehearsing every aspect of the launch and landing as well as the experiments they would carry out while in space.

Parasailing training exercises are also part of the survival school at Vance Air Force Base. Here Ron McNair prepares to be towed by a pickup truck in order to simulate a parachute glide. August 1978

During a three-day water survival course at Homestead Air Force Base in Florida, astronaut trainees learn the proper measures to take in the event of an ejection from an aircraft over water. In this exercise Ron McNair, wearing full survival gear, grabs a life raft and waits for a helicopter to retrieve him. August 1978

*Parasailing training is also part of the water survival course at Homestead Air Force Base. In this exercise a small motorboat will pull Guy Bluford and his parachute over the water, again simulating the glide of a parachute. August 1978*

*During water survival school astronaut trainees practice jumping into water with a parachute on, releasing themselves from their parachutes, and being rescued. Here, Guy Bluford takes part in an exercise that simulates a helicopter retrieval following a parachute landing in water. A lift device with an electric winch pulls Guy out of the water as a helicopter would were a water landing ever necessary. August 1978*

# Liftoff

## *Black Stars in Orbit*

**A**FTER FIVE YEARS OF TRAINING AND WORK AT NASA, Guy Bluford was assigned a place on the third mission of the Space Shuttle *Challenger,* STS-8. This historic mission took place from August 30 to September 5, 1983. The crew included five people—Commander Dick Truly, Pilot Dan Brandenstein, and Mission Specialists Dr. William Thornton, Dale Gardner, and Guy Bluford.

*The day that we flew, we got up at ten o'clock at night, we had breakfast, and at about midnight we went out to the pad. And I remember that it was dark and there was lightning and lots of rain, and I knew that there were an awful lot of people out there to watch this thing.*

—GUY BLUFORD

Isaac Gillam, now a senior vice president with OAO Corporation, an aerospace and information systems contractor, was director of Dryden's Flight Research Center at Edwards Air Force Base in California when STS-8 was launched. As the highest-ranking African American operations officer at NASA, Gillam was responsible for

*In the hours before the launch of STS-8 on August 30, 1983, a dramatic lightning storm brightens the night sky over the Kennedy Space Center in Florida.*

*Guy Bluford and the rest of the crew of STS-8 greet the crowd watching their departure for Launch Pad 39A at the Kennedy Space Center in Florida. August 30, 1983*

overseeing all performance tests of the Space Shuttle. He had been at NASA for twenty years and had participated in seventy or eighty launches, but always from the control room. He'd never seen a launch from the outside. NASA flew him to Florida, along with dozens of other VIPs, to witness the launch of this history-making space venture.

*It was raining, and the launch status was on hold because of the rain. But fortunately, the weather cleared and they resumed the countdown. And at ignition, the flash from the solid rocket boosters and the shuttle's main engines was just so incredibly bright that, it was around midnight, and now it's almost like daylight. And we heard that the flash from the ignition and liftoff of the mission had been seen as far north as North Carolina from the Florida launch. But it was a spectacular mission, and it was one of the high points in my life to have the opportunity to be present and to watch that launch.*

—ISAAC GILLAM

*The ride up was really a fabulous ride. . . . People tend to think that you're thrown back in your seat when you lift off. No, that wasn't the case. It was a smooth, gentle ride up. The experience of orbit was fantastic. Zero-G is really a unique experience.*

—GUY BLUFORD

Guy Bluford was the first African American to venture into space, to escape the gravity of earth, and to defy those who said blacks would never qualify to do so. Black people—and America—had come a long way since the days, forty years earlier, when the military and the United States government officially expressed their doubts that "Negroes" could ever learn to fly. We had come a long way since the days, twenty years earlier, when Captain Edward Dwight was told by an official then working in the astronaut training program that there would never be a "colored guy" in space. On August 31, 1983, President Reagan called from earth to the orbiting Space Shuttle to officially acknowledge the desegregation of space.

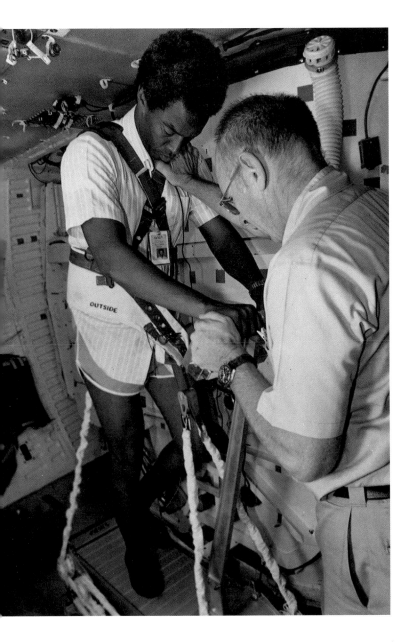

As part of their preparation for STS-8, Guy Bluford and fellow Mission Specialist Dr. William Thornton demonstrate an on-orbit experiment they plan to perform. The experiment involves a treadmill device designed by Dr. Thornton. July 1983

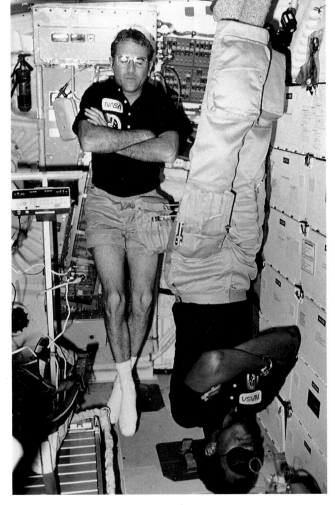

On board STS-8 Guy Bluford and Crew Commander Richard H. Truly stretch out for a Zero-G (zero gravity) rest.

*After landing the Space Shuttle* Challenger *at Edwards Air Force Base in California, the crew of STS-8 flew to the Johnson Space Center in Texas, where they had a postflight telephone conversation with President Ronald Reagan. September 1983*

*Guy, congratulations. You, I think, are paving the way for many others and you are making it plain that we are in an era of brotherhood here in our land, and you will serve as a role model for so many others and be so inspirational that I can't help but express my gratitude to you.*

—PRESIDENT RONALD REAGAN

Like the slaves in the myth who rose up like birds to claim their freedom, African Americans have risen from slavery and oppression to soar freely and as equals among the stars, triumphing in spite of great obstacles. There is a sort of poetic justice in that triumph: the runway at Edwards Air Force Base, the site where Major Robert Lawrence's F-104 Fighter crashed in 1967, was the site of the safe landing of the first black astronaut, Colonel Guion S. Bluford, sixteen years later.

When the Space Shuttle landed at 3:40 A.M. on September 5, there were about a thousand people there at Edwards Air Force Base waiting to welcome the crew home. The crew held a press conference during which the shuttle pilot, commander, and the other mission specialists expressed their pride in the *Challenger* and particularly Colonel Bluford, who had not only assisted with the lift-off and landing but had carried out the mission's main objective: the deployment of an Indian communications satellite. For his part, Colonel Bluford said that he was humbled by the presence of so many people who had come out to greet them at four o'clock in the morning. While realizing that his flight on the Space Shuttle would open the doors for other African Americans to get into the astronaut program, Guy Bluford magnanimously suggested that the great honor and the pride of this historic moment was one that everyone at NASA and all Americans could share in because it brought America that much closer to living up to its ideals of freedom, justice, and equality for all.

Further strides into space were made on February 3, 1984, when Dr. Ronald McNair's maiden voyage as a mission specialist on the *Challenger* flight STS-41B made him the second black American to rocket into the cosmos.

*Ron was always the curious type. I think it was back in 1958, when Russia first launched the spaceship, I think it was Sputnik, he would go outside and look up to the sky and he just couldn't understand how something that size could stay up in the sky. But the main reason that he continued to look up to the sky was because he got the feeling that maybe something may go wrong and that thing might fall, and he wanted to make sure he could see it coming down so it wouldn't fall on him. So he became real interested in space then, and I think from then on he must have had somewhere in the back of his mind that he was gonna play some part in space.*

—CARL McNAIR, RONALD McNAIR'S FATHER

*After the Terminal Countdown Demonstration Test, the final dress rehearsal for*
*the shuttle's blastoff, members of the crew of STS-41B, including Ron McNair*
(third from left), *practice emergency escape procedures at Launch Pad 39A.*

Although he was a civilian, Dr. Ronald McNair was an ideal
candidate for the space program's new breed of astronaut. With a
doctorate degree in physics from the Massachusetts Institute of
Technology (MIT), he had gone to work for Hughes Research Laboratories in California and before long had acquired an international
reputation as a leader in laser physics technology. The laboratories
of advanced scientific investigation were a long way from the cotton
and bean fields he sweated in as a child growing up in rural South
Carolina. For Ron McNair, the fields were just the first of many
testing grounds. "I gained qualities in those cotton fields," he once
said. "I got tough." For Ron McNair, working the fields was another
experience adding to his growing store of knowledge. Being well
rounded is as important a consideration in the astronaut selection
process as having the required degrees in the sciences. And Ron
McNair was a man of many talents. He was a fifth-degree black belt
karate instructor and a jazz musician.

On the *Challenger* flight STS-41B, McNair conducted micro-
gravity experiments, tested the new Cinema 360 camera, operated

*Ron McNair takes notes on one of the shuttle's experiments during STS-41B's eight-day flight. February 1984*

*Ron McNair playing his sax on board the shuttle during some of his off-duty time. February 1984*

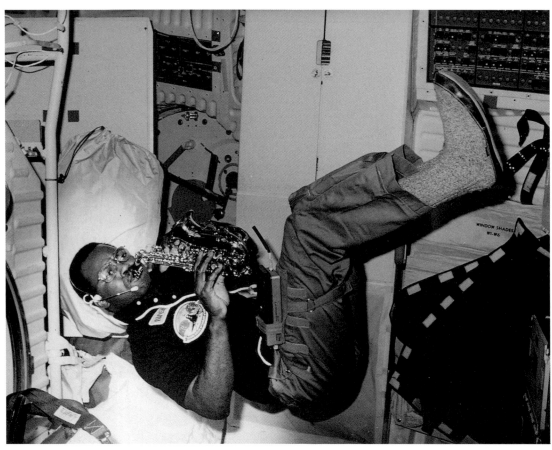

*Students at P.S. 5 in Brooklyn, New York, greet Ron McNair and celebrate his accomplishments.*

the shuttle's fifty-foot mechanical arm, and was responsible for the launch of a German communications satellite. Even beyond the satisfaction that comes with the accomplishment of their various tasks in space, all of the astronauts, black and white, seem to share in an experience that changes them profoundly—the experience of seeing how tiny and fragile the earth is.

*The only thing that he said about earth itself was that earth looked like a beautiful oasis, and he wished that the people there could live in peace as they were intended to. He hoped that someday they could all live together like that.*

—CARL McNAIR

At a press conference after that flight, Ron McNair unselfishly turned the spotlight away from himself to call attention instead to the tremendous value of the work being done by the shuttle program as a whole.

*The crew for STS-51B, led by Commander Robert F. Overmyer and Pilot Frederick Gregory, heads for the crew transfer van that will take them to the launchpad. Behind Overmyer and Gregory are Mission Specialist William E. Thornton and Payload Specialist Taylor G. Wang. April 29, 1985*

On April 29, 1985, when the *Challenger* lifted off on mission STS-51B carrying the billion-dollar Spacelab, Colonel Frederick Gregory became the first African American to actually pilot a Space Shuttle. For Colonel Gregory, as for most of the astronauts, this first flight was the most memorable.

*When the main engines lighted and ran as they were supposed to, and the solids lit and lifted off the pad gracefully . . . I suppose gracefully is a word that you might use . . . and then rolled over upside down, and then began to fly up the eastern coast of the United States, everything worked perfectly. I had seen lots of movies of space, I expected the skin to be ripped off my face and to be deafened by the tremendous sounds, the vibrations, but in fact it was a very, almost gentlemanly, docile, friendly environment during this first eight minutes of ascent.*

—FRED GREGORY

Once in orbit Colonel Gregory saw the world as very few others have seen it.

*As he guided the Space Shuttle* Challenger *around the earth, Fred Gregory
enjoyed views like this one of our planet. Most of the land shown here belongs to
Sudan, the largest nation in Africa; the curving river is the Nile.*

*You just get a marvelous view of the world from space. I was 190 miles
up. You see a lot of the world, and of course you're going around every
90 minutes, and so you see it very rapidly, and you see it over and over
again. And the thing that impressed me was that you could see Houston,
and then you'd see how really close Houston was to Mexico City, and
how close Mexico City was to South America, to Africa, to Russia.
Everything was right there. But the great thing about it was that, unlike
the Rand McNally maps, there were no state boundaries. You kind of
wondered from above as you looked down and as you passed over what
appeared to be city to city but was actually continent to continent, how
there could be any problems at all down there, because everybody was
everybody's neighbor.*

—FRED GREGORY

Piloting STS-51B was the culmination of a lifelong dream for Fred Gregory. Like Guy Bluford, Gregory built model airplanes as a kid and had decided early on that one day he would be a jet pilot. With a recommendation from New York Representative Adam Clayton Powell, Jr., he was able to get into the Air Force Academy. After graduation he began a career as a test pilot, which lasted until 1978 when he entered NASA for astronaut training.

Colonel Gregory's second flight marked another milestone for African Americans in the space program. On November 22, 1989, with the launch of the Space Shuttle *Discovery*'s mission STS-33, Colonel Gregory became the first African American commander of a Space Shuttle mission and crew. NASA had acknowledged once and for all that leadership ability is the only true criterion for leadership, and that race should never be a factor. Colonel Gregory was more than qualified. Not only had he served as the pilot on STS-51B, he had also made important contributions to the Space Shuttle's sophisticated technology, having redesigned the layout of its cockpit and instrumentation, making it more efficient and easier to fly for all shuttle pilots. In doing so, Frederick Drew Gregory continued in the proud tradition of African American innovators like his uncle, Dr. Charles Drew, the pioneering black surgeon who saved thousands of lives when he developed blood plasma and blood banks in the early years of World War II.

# Others Take Up the Challenge

**F**RED GREGORY, GUY BLUFORD, AND RON McNAIR were not merely tokens of integration. Others soon followed. Lieutenant Colonel Charles F. Bolden, Jr., had first considered applying for astronaut training in 1977 when NASA announced the Space Shuttle program. As a jet pilot with nearly three thousand hours of flying time, and as a scientist with degrees in systems management and electrical science, he had all the qualifications, but he also had some doubts because, in the past, NASA had always favored candidates with test pilot experience, at least for those astronaut candidates who were applying to be pilots of the Space Shuttle. Colonel Bolden was a pilot, but he had never been a test pilot. So, believing he would never be selected, he didn't even apply. Later, he learned that Guy Bluford, Fred Gregory, and Ron McNair were among the thirty-five members of the class of '78, the ones who were selected with that first group of shuttle astronauts. Bolden told himself that if he ever again got the chance to apply, he would give it his best shot. In the meantime, he became a test pilot, and in 1979 he got his second chance. He applied to NASA and was selected for astronaut training a year later. On his first flight into

*Charles F. Bolden, Jr., was selected as an astronaut candidate in May 1980.*

CHARLIE

NASA

*Charles Bolden standing in front of his father and younger brother at the Armed Forces Day at Fort Jackson, South Carolina*

*Charles Bolden mans the pilot's station on the flight deck as STS-61C prepares to reenter the earth's atmosphere. January 1986*

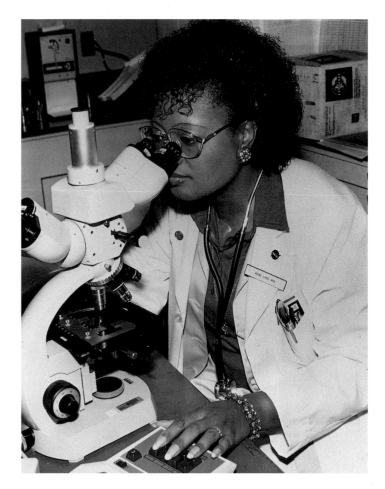

*Dr. Irene Long working at the Kennedy Space Center in Florida in 1986*

space on STS-61C, which lifted off January 12, 1986, Charles Bolden copiloted the Space Shuttle *Columbia*.

*It was absolutely breathtaking. It was everything I expected plus some. . . . I had done a lot of extra study to make sure I would recognize the different places we were going to see, the sequence they were going to come in, and I had taken it on as a personal undertaking to do as much photography of the continent of Africa as I could. I was just flabbergasted from the very beginning to find that it's just so massive, even from three hundred miles out in space, that there's just no way in the world that you can comprehend it all in the short span of, say, five or six days.*

—CHARLES BOLDEN

Throughout the 1970s and 1980s other black Americans continued to take part in NASA's work behind the scenes. Astronauts like Colonel Bolden were an inspiration for some of those who would join the space agency.

*Charles Bolden was probably one of the first astronauts I met. I was out in California, doing part of my aerospace medicine residency training, and I was told that he would be speaking at one of the junior colleges in San Jose. So I went to hear him speak and I passed a note to the person who was in charge saying that I was working in an aerospace medicine residency program and I'd like to meet him. After his speech he came over and talked to me and listened to my goals and aspirations and said, "You look like you'd be a nice person to work for NASA."*

—DR. IRENE LONG

When her medical training was complete, Dr. Long did join NASA. Today she is the acting director of the Biomedical Operations and Research Office at the Kennedy Space Center. She coordinates the human life science experiments for shuttle flights as well as the environmental monitoring and support for shuttle launches, landings, and day-to-day activities.

*The formal preflight portrait of the crew of STS-51L.* Left to right (front row):
*Michael J. Smith, Francis R. Scobee, and Ronald E. McNair;* (back row):
*Ellison S. Onizuka, Sharon Christa McAuliffe, Gregory Jarvis, and Judith A.
Resnik.*

On January 28, 1986, Ron McNair was preparing to take part in his second shuttle mission, STS-51L, aboard the Space Shuttle *Challenger.* The *Challenger's* launch was perhaps the most highly promoted of any shuttle launch. It was America in all its diversity; its crew was comprised of men and women, black, white, and Asian: Mission Specialist Ellison Onizuka; Pilot Mike Smith; the first teacher in space, Christa McAuliffe; Commander Dick Scobee; Payload Specialist Greg Jarvis; Mission Specialist Judy Resnik; and Mission Specialist Ron McNair. But what should have been the realization of a dream ended in tragedy. One minute and thirteen seconds after lifting off from Kennedy Space Center, the *Challenger* exploded in midair.

*Fred Gregory in the Mission Control Center moments after the Space Shuttle* Challenger *exploded in midair. January 28, 1986*

*After Ronald McNair's tragic death, New York City honored him by naming a street in Harlem after him. Left to right: Posing with the new street sign before it was mounted were Ronald McNair's mother and father, Manhattan Borough President David Dinkins, Ronald McNair's widow, Mayor Edward Koch, and Police Commissioner Benjamin Ward. October 1986*

*I feel that [Ron] must have had some sort of premonition. The day before that flight, he spoke with me on the telephone, and it seemed like he just didn't want to put that telephone down. He spoke with me a long, long time. And he said, "I hope they get this thing off the ground so I can get back and finish raising my children." My other boys and I had gone down for the launch, and after several postponements, we decided that we would go back to Atlanta, because we were under the impression that they were going to cancel this thing out. I went to sleep after I got home, and when I woke up, I woke up to the tapes [the videotaped replay of the accident]. First I thought it was one big horrible dream. But, if you recall, they continued to show those tapes over and over again, and I realized that dreams don't repeat like that.*

—CARL McNAIR

For more than two and a half years after the *Challenger* disaster, no shuttle missions were launched. But recruitment and training continued, and in September 1988 the launches resumed. Today, a renewed determination to pursue space exploration is the legacy left by the *Challenger* crew. Fred Gregory, Guy Bluford, and Charles Bolden have all flown missions since the *Challenger* disaster. And new astronaut candidates continue to join the ranks at NASA. Dr. Mae Jemison applied to NASA just before the *Challenger* explosion. But the disaster prompted NASA to suspend the astronaut training program until an investigation could determine what had gone wrong. Dr. Jemison is a licensed physician who holds degrees in chemical engineering and Afro-American studies. She also studied dance in school, and she speaks Swahili, Japanese, and Russian. Before applying to NASA Dr. Jemison had already had an exciting career as a young doctor working with the Peace Corps in West Africa. Some might have been dissuaded from joining the astronaut training program following the *Challenger* tragedy, but Dr. Jemison was determined to become an astronaut. When training at NASA resumed, she immediately renewed her application and in 1986 it was accepted by NASA and she entered the astronaut training program.

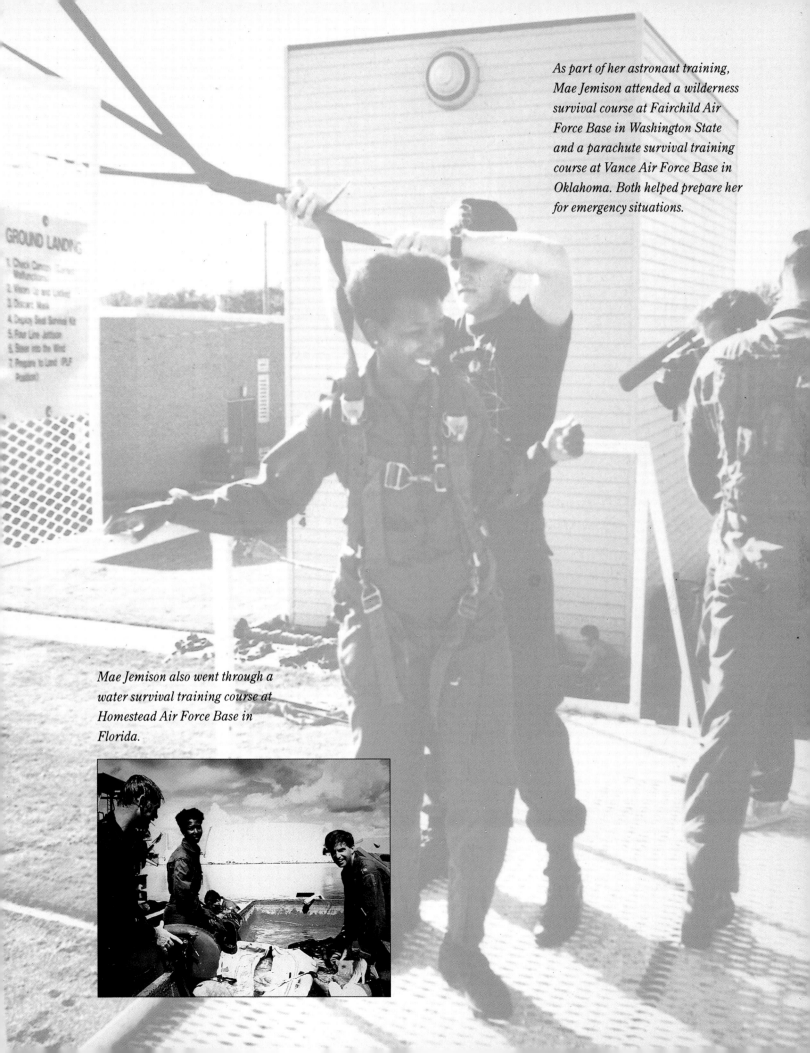

As part of her astronaut training, Mae Jemison attended a wilderness survival course at Fairchild Air Force Base in Washington State and a parachute survival training course at Vance Air Force Base in Oklahoma. Both helped prepare her for emergency situations.

Mae Jemison also went through a water survival training course at Homestead Air Force Base in Florida.

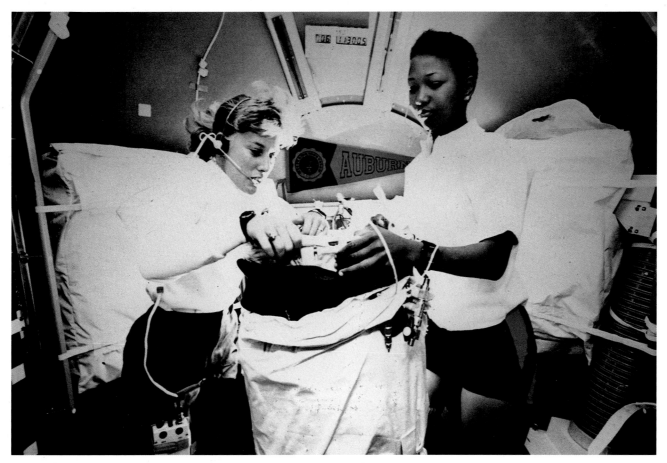

*Mae Jemison and fellow Mission Specialist N. Jan Davis prepare to test a lower body negative pressure apparatus as part of an experiment on board the* Endeavour. *September 1992*

*I always assumed I would go into space ever since I was a little girl. I would have applied to be an astronaut if there had never been a single person going into space.*

—MAE JEMISON

Six years after joining NASA, traveling on STS-47, Dr. Jemison fulfilled her childhood dream and became the first African American woman to travel into space. Her history-making flight was an important post-*Challenger* event.

One of the things Dr. Jemison experimented with on her flight was the use of biofeedback techniques to reduce space sickness. Space sickness is similar to seasickness, and most astronauts experience some form of it during their first couple of days in space.

*The crew of STS-47 on board the shuttle during their eight-day mission.*
*Left to right (front row): N. Jan Davis, Mark C. Lee, Mamoru Mohri, Mae C.*
*Jemison; (back row): Curtis L. Brown, Jr., Jerome Apt, and Robert L. Gibson.*
*September 1992*

Floating around upside down and every which way can take some getting use to. Astronauts can use a technique called biofeedback to control some of the symptoms of space sickness. By concentrating on their respiration, heart rate, and skin temperature, they can bring them within normal limits. If they are hyperventilating, they can concentrate on calming their breathing. It takes practice, but they can even learn to control their heart rate and other bodily processes in the same way.

After the successful completion of STS-47, Dr. Jemison took a leave from NASA in order to accept a fellowship to teach a course in space technology and developing countries at Dartmouth College in Hanover, New Hampshire. Her course attracted more women and minorities than any other undergraduate course in engineering in Dartmouth's history.

*Mission Specialist Bernard Harris and German Payload Specialists Ulrich Walter and Hans Schlegel at the Kennedy Space Center, preparing to take part in a dress rehearsal for the launch of STS-55. February 1993*

African Americans, Hispanics, Asian Americans, and women are all better represented in the astronaut corps of the 1990s because of the brilliance of the few black stars at NASA in the 1960s, 1970s, and 1980s. The number of minority applications for astronaut training has grown as more minority students have begun to feel confident about pursuing math and science courses in school. In 1993 the astronaut corps included Hispanics and Asian Americans such as Sidney Gutierrez, Ellen Ochoa, and Franklin Chang-Diaz; and fifteen women, among them, Eileen Collins, the first female pilot at NASA. African Americans such as Dr. Bernard A. Harris, Jr., a licensed physician, and Winston E. Scott, a commander in the United States Navy, continue to join the elite corps of black stars in orbit. For them, as for the enslaved Africans of our folklore, freedom has wings.

*Mission Commander Charles Bolden talking to amateur radio operators on earth from the flight deck of the Space Shuttle* Atlantis *on April 2, 1992*

*People always ask me, "What are we going to discover?" I don't know. I don't have any idea. If I knew, we wouldn't need to go. That's one of the exciting parts about spaceflight, just the prospect of what's going to come out that you never even dreamed of before.*

—CHARLES BOLDEN

# About the Authors

KHEPHRA BURNS grew up in Compton, California, where his father, who had been a Tuskegee Airman, ran a business at a small airport offering charter flights, instruction, and aircraft maintenance and repair during the 1960s. Every day after school and all day on Saturdays Khephra swept the hangar floor, washed airplanes, and later helped to build and repair them. His father told him stories about his adventures as a young Tuskegee pilot, and when Khephra was eleven his father began to teach him how to fly planes as well.

A few years after Khephra graduated from college, he began a career as a freelance writer. Over the years Khephra had the chance to travel around the world and to work with a wide variety of fascinating people; he wrote everything from scripts for television, advertising copy, and liner notes for recording artists including Miles Davis and Nancy Wilson, to speeches and columns for *Essence* and *Omni* magazines. In 1983, while attending a convention of the Tuskegee Airmen with his father, he met documentary filmmaker Bill Miles, and they agreed that one day they would work on a project together.

WILLIAM MILES grew up during the 1930s in a tenement building just behind Harlem's famous Apollo Theater in New York City. During his childhood Bill got to know Doll Thomas, the projectionist at the Apollo. He spent hours with Pops, as he called Thomas, watching the Apollo's feature films and learning how to thread films through the projector, how to rewind films, and how to scrape and splice them when they broke.

When Bill was seventeen Pops told him about Sterling Films, a new company on Fifty-seventh Street that was planning to rent out adventure films, travelogues, science films, and features to the television stations opening up across the country. The company was looking for a film inspector to label all the films in its library and to check them for damage as they went out and came back; Bill got the job.

During the nineteen years that Bill worked at Sterling he thought about films he would like to make. In 1965 he finally began the research that would lead to *Men of Bronze,* his first film, which told the story of the all-black regiment that fought with the French army during World War I. A film on the history of Harlem and another on blacks in the American military soon followed.

When Bill met Khephra Burns he was already thinking about making a film about black astronauts, and in 1986, with Khephra joining him as the screenwriter, Bill began researching *Black Stars in Orbit.* Over the course of five years Bill and Khephra visited NASA facilities in Texas and Florida, interviewed black astronauts and their families, and pieced together the exciting but unsung story of America's black astronauts. In early 1990 their documentary, *Black Stars in Orbit,* was finished and premiered on public television stations throughout the country. Three years later Khephra and Bill decided to tell the same story in a book. Using the research and the interviews they had done for the film as well as new research about some exciting developments at NASA—Mae Jemison had flown on her first mission since the release of the film, and Bernard Harris and Winston Scott had joined the astronaut training program—they wrote this book.

# Index